UNDERCLIFF

By the Same Author

A BRAVERY OF EARTH
READING THE SPIRIT
SONG AND IDEA
POEMS, NEW AND SELECTED
BURR OAKS
SELECTED POEMS

★

With Selden Rodman

WAR AND THE POET
An Anthology

UNDERCLIFF

POEMS
1946–1953

Richard Eberhart

1953

OXFORD UNIVERSITY PRESS

NEW YORK

FIRST PUBLISHED 1953

PRINTED IN GREAT BRITAIN

With
Old and New
Affection
for
My
Two
Gretchens

Contents

I

vii

Contents

II

III

viii

Contents

Acknowledgments

GRATEFUL acknowledgment is offered to the following publications where some of the poems in this book have appeared: *Accent; A Little Treasury of American Poetry; A Little Treasury of Modern Poetry; American Letters; Botteghe Oscure* (Rome); *Contemporary Poetry; Epoch; Glass Hill; Kavita* (Bombay); *Mid-Century American Poets; New Directions; New World Writing; Nine* (London); *Poetry, A Magazine of Verse; Poetry Ireland; Poetry Quarterly* (London); *Quarterly Review of Literature; The Beloit Poetry Journal; The Dartmouth Alumni Magazine; The Hudson Review; The Kenyon Review; The New Yorker; The Sewanee Review; The Tiger's Eye; The University of Kansas City Review; The Virginia Quarterly Review; The Western Review; The Wind and the Rain* (London); *Voices; Wake.*

"An Herb Basket" was first published by The Cummington Press, Cummington, Massachusetts in 1950.

PART I

INDIAN PIPE

Searching once I found a flower
By a sluggish stream.
Waxy white, a stealthy tower
   To an Indian's dream.
   This its life supreme.

Blood red winds the sallow creek
   Draining as it flows.
Left the flower all white and sleek,
   Fainting in repose.
   Gentler than a rose.

Red man's pipe is now a ghost
   Whispering to beware.
Hinting of the savage host
   Once that travelled there.
   Perfume frail as air.

slow moving

*nature remant
same
while man
kills self*

13

'GO TO THE SHINE THAT'S ON A TREE'

Go to the shine that's on a tree
When dawn has laved with liquid light
With luminous light the nighted tree
And take that glory without fright.

Go to the song that's in a bird
When he has seen the glistening tree,
That glorious tree the bird has heard
Give praise for its felicity.

Then go to the earth and touch it keen,
Be tree and bird, be wide aware
Be wild aware of light unseen,
And unheard song along the air.

WHAT IF REMEMBRANCE?

When I am lying under
A roof of green grass
That trembles when the thunder
And the white rain pass

And all my meaning gone
In the rhythmic turn of earth,
Senseless under the lawn
Even when grass takes birth

What if remembrance should come
Into the earth of my brain
And all my being plumb — *sealed with lead*
Again
Pain?

15

CHANT OF THE FORKED LIGHTNING

Let us break the cities down
Through pulses' feel
To a metaphysical town
Where love is real.

By the sweeping sea
Of old Mont St. Michel
Eat a weeping tea
For all that's gone: allons

By the rattling Bear
Sleep in the arms of Psyche,
A diamond on the finger,
And suit of a faun.

By the eternal Zoo
Hear the murderous caw
And upshot of it all,
Give a hand to how-de-do.

Go to the babbling spring ferns
They are learning
And on the mountain tops
The ice is burning,

Go to the shark sea shoals
Where the fight's on;
And back to pastures new
Where the fable's done.

Go to the fork of lightning
In the fork of lightning lie,
To that holy hierarchy
Of what you'll ever, never be.

Sometimes the longing for death,
Imaginative death, comes hard.
Not the unimaginable, last gasp,
But lift to supernatural love.

And sometimes death is achieved
In the visionary place of the mind,
New life, painful no more,
Where hope does not need to deter us.

Is it for this, most personal, most secure
Life turns, in goodness, and in evil
To tear our wits out of our wills
To its built, tremendous godhead?

ONE WAY DIALOGUE

Nothing is intractable in imagination.
There is an Idea in Heaven of to kiss.
Desire is the fruition of itself,
Love is the language of 'as if.'

Height is lost in its own obscurity,
Wishes the delirious air
Of feeling without loss of feeling,
The intangible tangible there.

O do not think to lose yourself
O do not wish to escape
The richness of the individual self
Or find yourself in another's shape.

We are locked in the individual—
All the delirium of the air
Will not extrude the basic sense
Of self found no otherwhere.

For though we give ourselves completely
It is only to find ourselves the more,
And though we tremble to touch the Host
It is the flesh that closes fast the door.

18

AT NIGHT

metonymy [✓]

dead {
In the <u>dust</u> are my father's beautiful <u>hands</u>,
In the <u>dust</u> are my mother's eyes.
}
Here by the shore of the ocean standing,
Watching: still I do not understand.

Love flows over me, around me,
Here at night by the sea, by the sovereign sea.

Gone is that bone-hoard of strength;
Gone her gentle motion laughing, walking. *dead*

Is it not strange that disease and death)
Should rest, by the <u>undulant</u> sea? } 3 *irony*
singing

And I stare, rich with <u>gifts</u>, alone,
life   earthly-irony

Feeling from the sea those <u>terrene</u> presences,
My father's hands, my mother's eyes.

19

REALITY! REALITY! WHAT IS IT?

Christ, I have walked around your erection,
The Cross, that begot, upon a sky of prayer
A billion men, devoted in humility
And I have denied You, a yea-sayer

Yet in pride and ignorance in sin
Too heady, too extreme, too willing
The breadth of the worlds I have travelled in
Should give me insight into all religions; who, milling

In the grips of poverty, or of sexuality,
In sophistication, or in imagination
Have sought all men as my division
And considered the first truth tragedy

Christ, though I should die tonight in hells
Of torture of struggle yet unknown to me
I sense the perfect and queer impetus of my blood
The sole guide upon this helpless flood

Of the light of the life I asked never for
And the triumph of glory I have known
The holiness of death I sheer affirm
And the harsh beatitudes of cruelty

O stars, glitterers, mere salt
Or chemic stuff students sometimes tell
Though great beyond measurement, and ants so small
There are human beings in the world still

Whose passion, rich as the superb pearl
Of holy love they fling in the mire of the real
Burns at the white heat of realization
Of the destruction it is to feel;

20

And whose cleft natures destroy themselves
Caught in the flaw of their self's largess,
Plungers of the earth's infinitudes
Who most because they deny, cry Yes

O Christ of Easter, impossible Man, Lord, and God
I, cold geographer, map Your clear estate
As one sentient, yet a prisoner, clashing Thy
Cymbal in the gliding sound of my dying,

Christ of Christ, what are you, beast or God,
Must I deny that sweat upon that cross?
Must I affirm what is not whatever I am,
Christ, Christ! reality! reality! what is it?

A LOVE POEM

I am the lightness that I know
And I am the terror that I seem;
The taint, the question, and the dream.
Perhaps you are also.

When the wind blows, and trees shake,
I think there is some comfort in them;
Else, in the silence of contemplation,
All harry me and my mind take.

Therefore, what I am interested in
Is the anatomy of time;
Whether there is anything substantial
In the world and flesh we are in.

But Love told me the answer,
In the moist garden, when the worms were out;
Love evaded the painful question,
When my eyes were a green dancer.

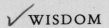

WISDOM

It is the secret voices of the grave
Speak to our meanings;
Our stumbling lives
Are summed by silences relieved.

Through the thin air of night,
Through hieratical *consecrated* years,
Against the boast of reason,
From death comes our pure sustenance.

It is these secret voices, the holy
Voices of the loved, the dead
That lend to us our meaning,
As we tread the road of human folly.

Ours is the loss, not theirs, who lie
In fields we cannot know,
Of silence, or of grace
Incalculable, death overthrown.

Not among living presences
Where suns of power presume
Is there their golden room
Of light where the human is the true.

Not by chance, not by fate
Is man significant;
He is not blessed
By earthly fortune or by fame.

And his *primary* primordial misery
Is that dark key
By which seeing
He measures the claims of vanity.

23

It is the secret voices of the grave
Hallow our pilgrimage;
From youth to age
They hint alone at what we are.

They come mysteriously, the voices,
And the heart knows
When they burgeon
Immutability, by mutable laws.

They are the heart's cleft desire
And sums of us,
Inscrutable
In inscrutability.

Learn from the potent voices
What you shall never know;
When time turns,
You will wear the truth of the grave.

And life's jangle, life's passion
With centuries will be
Whisper in midnight
Over the grave, ineluctably.

Love will be time
Dreaming of God;
The vast purpose
Will whisper on.

GOD AND MAN

My grandmother said I was an atheist *— loses identity*
God said I was a man.
My father took me by the hand,
My mother vanished in a mist.

In the rich stores of the ether
The future was seen as the past,
Flesh was aerial prescience, *foresight*
And the devil was seen last.

In time you have no grandmother
For ancient earth recedes.
Your father and your mother go,
But God says, you are a man. *not a corpse.*

Between budding leaf and blue sky
Angels of mercy were spreading,
Like bees around the cider-press
Diffusing this blood with murmurousness.

The angels were the archetypes.
Would go away while devils overcame
Time, and chased the crooked years,
You still lusting after evil.

Evey one a father and a mother has
And every one more ancient staffs,
Yet all lose even loss itself
When God says, you are Man.

For man precedes his knowledge
Aroused within his variant myth,
A stalwart, fiery with animus
Whose death is only another dream.

25

And God has the deep justice,
And God has the last laugh.
To be God God needs man
As man needs God to be man.

THE POET-WEATHERVANE

A fresh breeze stirred from the East.
As were percussives in the open air
His cheek,
In love with murmurousness,
Faced
To the East into that fair pressure.

Or if from the West
A salt oppressive movement
Archly came,
He, subtle of reach,
Turned avidly to face it,
Searching there.

So perfectly he waxed upon his point
It was as if,
Anticipating
Each veering of the wind,
He drew them to him,
Hypnotist.

No history of ideas,
But swiftly
He turned by law
Into the eye of truth,
And it seemed to him
In freedom, for always

Without preoccupation,
Sheerly balanced,
He pointed into the wind,
A signature
Instinct with decision,
Willingly written.

27

It was only in stilled air,
In death–like stillness,
Without animation, or doctrine,
That he stood
Helpless, pointless,
In an ague of despair.

This myth let all then see, and draw
The damage of the centuries.
It used to be an inner animus *animation*
Could make men free;
Our modern minds determine
Weathercock certainty.

THE HORSE CHESTNUT TREE

Boys in sporadic but tenacious droves
Come with sticks, as certainly as Autumn,
To assault the great horse chestnut tree.

There is a law governs their lawlessness.
Desire is in them for a shining amulet *charm against evil spirits*
And the best are those that are highest up.

They will not pick them easily from the ground.
With shrill arms they fling to the higher branches,
To hurry the work of nature for their pleasure.

I have seen them trooping down the street
Their pockets stuffed with chestnuts shucked, unshucked.
It is only evening keeps them from their wish.

Sometimes I run out in a kind of rage
To chase the boys away: I catch an arm,
Maybe, and laugh to think of being the lawgiver.

I was once such a young sprout myself
And fingered in my pocket the prize and trophy.
But still I moralize upon the day

And see that we, outlaws on God's property,
Fling out imagination beyond the skies,
Wishing a tangible good from the unknown.

And likewise death will drive us from the scene
With the great flowering world unbroken yet,
Which we held in idea, a little handful.

THE TOBACCONIST OF EIGHTH STREET

I saw a querulous old man, the tobacconist of Eighth Street.
Scales he had, and he would mix tobacco with his hands
And pour the fragrance in a paper bag.
You walked out selfishly upon the city.

Some ten years I watched him. Fields of Eire
Or of Arabia were in his voice. He strove to please.
The weights of age, of fear were in his eyes,
And on his neck time's cutting edge.

One year I crossed his door. Time had crossed before.
Collapse had come upon him, the collapse of affairs.
He was sick with revolution,
Crepitant with revelation.

And I went howling into the crooked streets,
Smashed with recognition: for him I flayed the air,
For him cried out, and sent a useless prayer
To the disjointed stones that were his only name:

Such insight is one's own death rattling past.

SEA SCAPE WITH PARABLE

A practical hand at catching fish is necessitous;
Mark the sociability, as in the fish themselves
Who dance, pronouce, waltz, or as it were rollick
In close presses of their solidarity toward Weir Cove,
A natural phenomenon. God, I suppose, sends them.
And the fishers, drawn from hamlet, farm, and dock,
Push out their various vessels and elenctic gear,
At a sign come quickly to the holy mackerel.

These are dancing on the water, with professional ease.
Are cast prophetic nets, with a glance cast at the weather.
Jubilation sits in the eyes of old and young: a catch.
It is as yare as anything in the book of sea lore,
The time right, wind and wave crucially conspiring.
The gulls, above, pervade the sky; far off the ospreys
Sit meanly on their rocks, barbarous, meditative.
It is an event social, of bulging, conclamant waters,
An exercise in a precise corner of the right sea.

It is not to speak of ghostly scavengers,
Not in the sky can be seen absolute integers
To the contemplative sense: oilskinned men
Traverse a shining field of water like toed dancers;
Time the skilled fisherman they do not see,
Nor feel their bones consecrated to the rocky walls,
Nor flesh reduced by rough force to everlasting lightness.

The work goes on as it always has; some hours of sun
And wind, and jockeyings of the ropes, calculations
Of stress, a lively timing, expert arraignment
Of the mass, and finally the huge haul comes in.
The shining victims, lost multitudinously
Are hoisted and shovelled into the capacious holds.
 As silently as fish are vigorously together
 Swimming, directed by the laws that govern them,

Who come this time of year to this defeating place,
The fishermen veer off and fall away at eventide,
Rich with big increase, leaving a vacant sea.
Which, seen in retrospect, as if without event,
Is full of a wide and charming serenity.

So by the inevitable analogy, are fished
Souls by the Fisher King, who with the net of time
Searches them into the silent bin of death,
Yet ever vigorous swarms of men laugh with the living.

It is true that sometimes, due to some error in man,
Some clumsy misadventure, the whole lot gets away,
And he goes back to land without his edibles,
Mocked, disenchanted, hugging his big stupidity,
Awaiting another try at the fabulous oncome.

Yet who would say, in all philosophy,
That the Master of Mankind errs and is vain?
Who would disallow the Fisher's victory,
As we drink our spirit in the haven halls of men?

SEALS, TERNS, TIME

The seals at play off Western Isle
In the loose flowing of the summer tide
And burden of our strange estate—

Resting on the oar and lolling on the sea,
I saw their curious images,
Hypnotic, sympathetic eyes

As the deep elapses of the soul.
O ancient blood, O blurred kind forms
That rise and peer from elemental water:

I loll upon the oar, I think upon the day,
Drawn by strong, by the animal soft bonds
Back to a dim pre-history;

While off the point of Jagged Light
In hundreds, gracefully, the fork-tailed terns
Draw swift esprits across the sky.

Their aspirations dip in mine,
The quick order of their changing spirit,
More freedom than the eye can see.

Resting lightly on the oarlocks,
Pondering, and balanced on the sea,
A gauze and spindrift of the world,

I am in compulsion hid and thwarted,
Pulled back in the mammal water,
Enticed to the release of the sky.

THE CANCER CELLS

Today I saw a picture of the cancer cells,
Sinister shapes with menacing attitudes.
They had outgrown their test-tube and advanced,
Sinister shapes with menacing attitudes,
Into a world beyond, a virulent laughing gang.
They looked like art itself, like the artist's mind,
Powerful shaker, and the taker of new forms.
Some are revulsed to see these spiky shapes;
It is the world of the future too come to.
Nothing could be more vivid than their language,
Lethal, sparkling and irregular stars,
The murderous design of the universe,
The hectic dance of the passionate cancer cells.
O just phenomena to the calculating eye,
Originals of imagination. I flew
With them in a piled exuberance of time,
My own malignance in their racy, beautiful gestures
Quick and lean: and in their riot too
I saw the stance of the artist's make,
The fixed form in the massive fluxion.

I think Leonardo would have in his disinterest
Enjoyed them precisely with a sharp pencil.

THE LOOK

At the last hour, before the transition,
The true grain of life appears;
The bells, the flowers, the feint of youth,
The stride of character.

It is before the departure
The sensate message comes,
Rites of pain,
And then there is only the dream.

O bells, O flowers, O stripe of character
That state with absolute regard!
One look of life's loose years
Was vision, and then that look was gone.

And night came on upon the marble lawn
And the stars were as they were before.

And Mayan and Incan temples blent
Their lavish colours with dance pageantry.

And you, in jungles of awareness,
Will think to live in after-time,
Who live to gather up the look
You saw, from years that dream.

BAUDELAIRE

Some implacable work I planned
That had the humanity of all Europe.
Against the conspiracy of the world
I set the chances of my integrity.

Man is not made to master the world
I found in twenty years of effort.
While my zeal with inexorable thought inclined
My flesh contracted, my blood turned sour.

The weaker Time the Enemy made me
The stronger became my imagination.
The body's lust became the lust of the mind,
I would conquer by the force of pure mind.

Poor Soul! Pure mind was another fiction,
As age reared its victimizing spectacle.
I caught a flame from Greece and Rome,
From sweet France and melancholy England.

Why, with all the sins of old Europe,
Wars, ravage, strife, and out of these
The vaults I climbed of lithe cathedrals,
Was I locked in violence and stupidity?

I saw the voyage and the meaning,
Boredom, despair, and every vanity,
False gods or true, passion, clarity,
I wrote in order the blood of Lethe.

One lesson loathe to learn or teach
I was, for all the works I penned
Of learning and humanity:
Love, the source, I failed to honour.

OEDIPUS

Oedipus should have found exit from his dilemma:
Blinding of the eyes does not impove the insight.
How dark and magnificent were the Greeks! How
Their melancholy rings down the years to this day,

Rings in my ears the wail of the man going blind,
As universal blood streams through the firmament.
Not to unravel the doom but to accept it
Is even what I did when first I saw him bleeding.

Oedipus should have had a will to escape it.
He should have been able to outspan the plot.
Is there no perception to pierce through Fate?
Is nothing bright in man to dispel Destiny?

In barking and brittle light, in the antique air
I see him in the universal drench,
Fate that is stronger than the soul of man,
Destiny that rides us like a whirlwind.

INDIAN SUMMER

I saw my days as passionate integers,
They leaped upon the wind as leaves
Leaping upon the wind; not Spring leaves
Fixed; I see them all as Autumn leaves.

It is the season of my mellowest appetite,
And germane to my soul; cruel times forgot,
Unvexing, the joyful. Plain days unspecified.
The clear enchantment of dry exhalations!

I would speak a word deep and pure,
Pure and deep, deep, deep and pure.
And these Autumnal days speak for me here—
Realization—else what is Autumn for?

I think the Indian Summer's long regard
Flanks all the days with resonance—
That I shall never be more richly blessed
Than I am breathing in it now.

✓ ORDER AND DISORDER

A passion came to me in the form of order,
To order all things in the mind.
Seek then frenzy, the foliating blood, then,
Seek the schisms of the stars, the will.

And did the passion come from order's self?
I heard in the wind the falling of a leaf.
And as the night's weak eye bore down on mine,
Was I its killer, was I its thief?

Strange things go on in the subtle night,
In the darkness the ages murmur and tremble.
Plato conceives, and Aristotle measures,
Buddha thinks deep, and Christ is burning white.

Each is an order, but each is a blight.
I feel my bood abounding, massive in darkness.
Each was an order, but each its order closing
In total harmony, save only Christ.

And the passion was a wild air of night,
It was a violation of the mind in its order,
A tumult, a transgression, ingression,
Christ's blood the strain in truth's disorder.

FORMS OF THE HUMAN

I wanted to be more human
For I felt I thought too much
And for all the thinking I did—
More rabbits in the same hutch.

And how to be more human, I said?
I will tell you the way, I said.
I know how to do it, I said.
But what I said was not what I did.

I took an old garden hoe
And dug the earth, and planted there,
Not forgetting the compost too,
Three small beans that one might grow.

Three grew tall, but one was wild
So I cut off the other two,
And now I have a wild bean flower
The sweetest that ever grew.

THAT FINAL MEETING

It is what you see on a death-bed
That you cannot ever understand.
The strangeness of the cumulation,
Against which nothing can be said.

It is this universal silence *metonymy*
And the cold serenity of mind
After the vast abuse of life
That folds us all in mystery.

It is not what you can do or say,
Not any tenderness, or memory,
But only the brute recognition,
The bareness, the sting.

SOUL'S REACH

Poverty said, I am in love.
Love said, I grow gray.
I watched them with my heart
And my mind fled away.

Heart, be patient, heart,
Mind, O infant mind, stay.
Until I can cry Yea
I can only say Nay.

CHILIASM — *Christ will return to rule*

When I look into the (mountain air — *heavens*)
God looks into me;
That is my statement,
That is my authority.

But when I dive into the sea — *hell*
And swim in choking wrath *(cant breathe)* — *sad*
By the throat Satan shakes me,
Shakes me. My life he has.

So when I stand on the sea shore
Looking into the mountains,
Looking into the sea,   *between heaven & hell*
God and the Devil are in me. *can be good or evil*

I am Love and I am Wrath. *God* *Satan*

PART II

Four-thirty in the morning,
The coldest morning in late October.
Mechanical,
I stepped into clothes sprawled at hand before.
Effigies of tenuous waking dreams
Walked with me down the stairs,
Hardly realizations,—subtle separate sensations.
Chill air, and congealed skin,
So wake the mouth and hair.
I walked to work, Times Square
And all buildings little comprehended.
Unreality again, all this steel,
Height, lights: my feet alone know.
The usual stragglers pass. Strugglers?
Or only I? Or not I, they? Is
Nothing palatable but figs and coffee?
Then skirted along, briskly
Forty Second Street, to the west.
Head down, wind like a wire whip
Trying from neck to chest. Fingers
My collar closing are like a python's mouth.
My thighs feel good,
Action always feels good.
Except contemplation's,
When feet run in the brain.
Tenth Avenue, newspapers asleep in humble blankets.
Why look back? or even forward?
Feet can tell. Ten minutes late
This morning; see, night opens
One shade to the morning. The stars merely
Are pin points; not as on the Indian Ocean,
To be waked, naked, warm,
On a hatch, when stars sigh goodnight.
Not very wary. Eleventh Avenue,
I came around the corner and there,

Above the seven box-like and lamp-lit
Shelves of the packing house,
Glared the visitant metallic moon,
Canny as a dead man's eye.
Taormina. God, floods of foam.
There's a plumber playing pipes in my guts,
It screeches. Escapeless, common feeling.
Vapour from the factory rose up
Against the cold and paling light,
But vanished lower than the moon's aura.
Why must it be thus with you, never
To find the one untormented integer.
Surprise moon, four-thirty moon,
Dead moon, so rich with our ecstasies.
My stomach's got the goose flesh: wind of thin whips.
Into Hell again. I'll one glance,
Two glance, let it go, slip the moon's pierce,
Or grow great with old ravage.

Until the din became immense and profound,
A living horror of common death,
Merciless, disjunctive, co-ordinate;
Until relativity made this equable, and
Rhythm was levelled with it, it had
No meaning but simple action, happening.
Only one in a hundred kicked;
Kicked violently, pathos-maker,
Leer-long, with every energy.
A hog became a living curve,
Drew itself convex, from the vertical
Imposition of the ankle shackle.
Everything in nature curves.
So with beauty also; but I never
Decided; or decided so many times,
I have no decision. Decisions
Are practical, they do not increase the soul.
The killer's face! He is baffled now,

Seems. Moment. He poises
The tip of the knife at the throat.
So little is life. He cannot make
The one swift entry and up-jab.
Curious copulation, death-impregnation.
How the blood flows out
Dark red in a full stream;
Or some hold theirs in, muscles so tense,
One minute, then bewildered they rush into panic,
Six or eight or maybe only four
Wild screams, or grunts that can't
Get through the blood. This one baffles:
Odd. The vibrating free leg's too quick
For the killer to catch it. Then,
With almost a solemn decision,
The life-taker jams the terrified animal
On to a side rail: three more wait, with
Din-horrific screeches. They are dispatched
With able, easy gesture,
Purposive intercourse!
When there is a pause in the chain,
His inevitable great hand swings round
(Belly to belly) the daring pig.
Still its agony increases,
So much vitality expended,
Every muscle expresses itself
Against imminent death.
A dramatic instant of pause.
Of course there is no hope. In
Some dark way I wish
Life were less terrible.
These are all people strung up,
You understand. Not one chance,
Not a single.
Nature wants no virginity:
Must wed and be dead.
Big purpose (pig purpose) is to be killed.

We hope the inevitable hand
(Splendid huge veins there, bright wet
Red to the elbow) will be stayed
From him, from us. What a magic instant,
The tip at the throat, a little jab
Into the skin unfelt, then the
Deft probe, the jugular, conception.
Thus! And the admirable God's creature
Dies powerfully screaming.
A show! A show!
Come see the big Negro stick pigs.
That one was rare, to kick against the pricks.
His enthusiasm was unwarranted,
As if he were not of his genus,
But had the life of genius.

This is a vast sadistic enterprise.
Good for us, times, to see and feel
Down into sixty men. They
Stand upon greasy benches, with sharp knives.
The endless chain is begun,
With guttural as-if-eating-bolts groaning.
It is the endless chain of their labour.
Chilled hogs appear at the end
(As in a Blake angels would
At 'per me si va tra la perduta gente').
What if they, too, were people,
Some other intelligence were using,
As are used, these carcases.
The earlier initiation,
Neophytes knowing their Achilles heel,
Their tragic flaw, heads downward to earth,
Great Mother! All dead by
Some Pig Intelligence butchering.
Guts ripped out, young women too,
Old men, after fresh bath in a hot tank
Scalding the hair off. Then the

50

Whole family, and cousins Kate, Bertha, Percy,
Strung up, as I said, by Achilles
His heel. Ripped down
From penis, or vagina, through navel
(Inside out) to chin or cancer of the throat.
Faces sliced off, see fantastic mirth,
Comedy of errors, tragedy of desires,
On expressions so quick-changing.
Intestines on moving tables,
The last humiliation of having
The insides examined. If foul,
Condemned. Skinned, fat cut off,
Around we go on the chain slow,
And a great knife down, once, through the spine;
The skull split open, brains given an airing,
At last. Pea-sized pituitary.
I said the chilled hogs appeared at the far end,
A Negro big as Amazon,
Amazing, cuts them down onto the belt.
A white man, next him, like a giant
Marionette, with titan thews and blows,
(Conditioned by recurring necessity)
Chops with one vast climax
Belly from loin. His body
Turns, shifts, turns, swerves,
The splendid toy,
Man full-strong and hale.
He loves his home's children.
Also alcohol. Plato's dead.
Butchers are told by their knuckles,
As poets are told by love.

On top, all storeys up, if you walk out
On the roof as if doing something,
There are the ships,
The lambent air burdened with life tunes,
Little screaming and quiet symphonies,

Even in New York. O tall beautiful,
No, not sails any more, nor Queequegs:
Yet not too sullen steel plows,
And carriage like health. The
Colour of intestines fascinates.
I saw lungs like mackerel sunsets in Haiphong;
Smooth bladders the
Shade of evening's amber rain;
Hearts as of New Mexican earth,
When wet; all very carnelian.

Why love so long the even, but almost
Deathy darkness, that wells
Into dawn over buildings:
Opaque quietude, such tonal,
One mode. Why love so strong.
Perhaps because gentleness
Looks real (like death).
And the sun, when he comes glaring,
Is pain unending. Wrap around me,
Shroud of the dawn almost:
The sun with his eye will put out mine.
Sweet universal sky, seen
Through the sesame-slit of a dirty lavatory,
Where I wash my hands of hates.

I pretend I am the young Goya,
Enjoying fallow and burnished,
There, polyglot faces. His the bigger
German's, with hands oily to match,
Of matchless golden aura, dark
Enough, as in Rembrandt, too
Solid to be eclectic, no Goya;
But smoothest tempered skin all
Health, an animal pleasure,
Let us rejoice. Undangerous he,
Regular, in simplicity, without

Pride but humble in muscles
And can say "aw right" almost American.

John, Czecho-Slovakian competent,
Bites his hand in a steel door.
Incoming truck's the gorge, bitter
Teeth, and no fault. Pitiful
O my John, like a different man
With mind bemused and maimed,
John like a boy almost whimpers,
Waits upon sympathy. Puffed
Hands under warm water tap.
Huge arms capable of
Two hundred pounds hold the hurt
Hand as it were a flower;
Or a dead something.

There is some mournful music,
Somewhere, I give myself into
The slow god. Like a man
Grasping at peace, maelstromed
In this fourmillante cite.
Until sombrely, lovingly I close
In the doleful scales my being.
It is a whole world of direct power,
Now, intangible, being
So in solitude, seeming powerless.
But while in the thick pleasure
Not any says: experience
Lives as at a sea's depth,
In its darkness, surrounded
By itself, by itself filled,
Tonal tropism. I am
My own tonal tropism. I am.
The something done by dense
Minor, no lyric, oneness,
One sound, and essence of being,

Being without the object, yet
So surely oneself in spite of it.
Accordance of sympathy,
Equilibrium of the tempo composed
Of disparate things.   All sorrow,
Let it be my shroud, in folds
Of music. Known in the heart's
Well, like standing in mud.

Embowelled again. Put the insides out.
This is a vast peristalsis.
Robbers dine on expectations,
In caves of hesitancies.
Sparse gigantic flecks of what might be snow;
Walk on murder trials to work. It is so cold;
Try over the buildings to the colder moon,
That same, for warmths, fires, flames of hell.
Not there, this dated night, can keep love
Out of mind, Sicilian singing.

In the lyric buoyance of this dull café,
She came into the café, walked to the back,
Sat with her back to the front
Of the room. The ugliest woman I'd
Ever laid eyes on,
Life to the viscera. Revulsion and vision spring.
Skin like malice, that makes her eyes unbearable.
Ripeness is gall. She spoiled my meal,
And a rat ran over my feet.

I thought they were all standing
Around like dead men,
So much physical life they had,
Who laboured among red substances.
They were dead men, so I mused
Among noises, silence the heat and
Cyclopean eye of vibrations,

Activity the opposite of whatever it is.
They were dead men, with big hands
Cooler-puffed, no life in them,
Continually I mused upon,
And amused me with this
Runlet of consciousness,
Confounded with the actual?
No life in them, but they were of life,
See still I fret about the mind.
But one might almost say their bodies thought,
In their honest and cool cells.

I have flung myself down into this pit.
Now they are all dead; statuesque
Stand these actors, these buildings
Building no more. Death I saw,
And wormed through it. And make fragment
Of the end of a time, when seethed
So thick the life, it knew not,
In savage complexity, modernity,
The harsh omnipotence of evil.

AESTHETICS AFTER WAR

(To A. Nykyforcza,
Student of Sighting.

The floating reticle became your eye,
You saw flashing battle,

You returned in the death lists.)

I PROPOSITIONS

Is the rose the same after it is seen?
Is it brighter if the seer has a blighted gall bladder?

If a poet is colour blind, either by nature,
Or say by choice,
So that his deep wish to see purple
Gives him constitutionally a purple world,
As the romanticist finds excess where others
Do not find it,
As the classical scholar finds the world more classical
Than any striking steel worker knows it,
As the aesthetician finds the world
An aesthete's paradigm, to whom then
The pleasure principle is the end of all,
Do the poet, the romanticist, the classicist, the aesthetician
By their profound aberration
Discover the true reality of nature?

What is the relation of aesthetics to philosophy?
Should there be any?
Is its branch an authentic olive tree?
If you contemplate the rose, do you have to think about it?
If you achieve a beatific state
In the contemplation of the rose
Are you loving wisdom?
Is it possible to achieve abstract purity,
The ultimate knowledge of the object rose,

Without a mystical infiltration?
Should an aesthetician wish to think?
Should a thinking aesthetician want to know God?
Will God appear in the ultimate stillness of the rose?

Keats confused, confounded two centuries
By ambivalent, ambiguous
Mating of truth with beauty.
Or are these absolutes safe in unattainability?
So that the searcher, as centuries ago,
May struggle, physically, logically, semantically,
Or by purposive derangement of the senses
To find them, being relatively certain
Their abstraction will inhere and remain
Long after his bones have turned to very earth?

What has the aesthetics to do with society?
Was the Italian airman crazy
When he saw aesthetic purity
In bombs flowering like roses a mile below?
He could not see nor feel the pain of man.
Our own men testify to awe,
If not to aesthetic charm,
On seeing man's total malice over Hiroshima,
That gigantic, surrealistic, picture-mushroom
And objectification of megalomania.
A world of men who butcher men
In the arsenical best interests of several states,
The modern warring maniacal man,
Is this world of men inimical
To the postulates of the study aesthetics?

II   INSTRUMENTS

There are many intricate pieces of workmanship,
Precise instruments like the Mark 18 Sight,

With a floating reticle and a fixed reticle,
The fixed being a circle of light with a cross at the centre,
The floating being eight brilliant diamond points of light
In a broken circle which enlarges and contracts
Framing the enemy wingspan, increasing
As the enemy plane comes nearer, grows larger,
Decreasing as it flies away, grows smaller,
The whole floating reticle a dream of beauty,
But accurate to a split second of gunfire,
Its gyroscopic precision solving all problems
Of boresight, the pursuit curve,
Of wind drift, range, of bullet pattern
So that as semi-automaton all the young gunner
Has to do is to frame the enemy plane
In this brilliant circle of light and blaze away.
This is one of a bewildering array of imaginations.
Radar, as another expression of ingenious invention,
In its excessive, but already dated modernity,
Only gives man what bats have used for centuries,
Whose vibrations, beyond the reach of the human ear,
Strike obstacles which echo back to warn the bat
Who instantly evades each thing that would harm,
Although he seems to us to employ erratic flight.

Warfare spurs man to electrify himself with technics
But never can the human be contraverted
And as the Mark 18 Sight is only the fastest
Eye in the fastest brain, the perfectly anticipatory one,
And as radar is only an equal intelligence
To the ancient, instinctive knowledge of the bat,
So mankind in his abrasive rigors
Constructing the mazes of his complex aircraft
Often unwittingly makes them look like huge
Beetles or other insects, and I have seen
Hundreds of Corsairs parked in the evening glow
Their wings folded back ethereal as butterflies.

If a floating reticle in an electrical sight,
If a radar screen with its surrealistic eeriness,
If an airplane poised on the ground like a butterfly
Are beautiful, is their beauty incidental?
Is it man's limitation that his mechanical creations
Perforce cannot escape from his manhood?
And that try as he will, his works are human
And never stray far from the functions of the natural?
The mystery is whether the object
Mystifies man,
Or whether the mysteriousness within man
Transubstantiates the object;
Whether the world is finally mysterious,
Or if the Deity has put a mystery in man.

III   THE PULL OF MEMORY

Each argument begets its counterpart,
Only in opposites the truth is human,
Intelligible, the shoemaker Boehme said.
I recall a steamer on the Pearl River
Slipping out from teeming Canton,
Hong Kong outward bound through swarming sampans,
The glow of the East, the intense hot day,
The swan sweep of the boat on swan-swept water,
The lull of the hours in the yellow afternoon,
I remember walking the deck
Watching the ritual of the opium eaters
Through glassless windows in the inner sanctum,
Sensing their subtle gestures and serene manners
Through the prolonged trance of the opium haze;
Then looking out, on the banks of the Pearl River
Ancient of days, and of centuries,
There stood a tall pagoda old as the memories of China.
So Buddha seemed in the soft air to dwell,
Incomparably indwelling, selfless and whole,
Without action, away from world's suffering.

And I was stolen in a trance
Of the pagoda like a jewel in ancient, shimmering air,
And of the mild-eyed Chinese recumbent after smoking,
Mysterious inducements of the suffusing scene.

In the East contemplation is a self-annihilation,
In the West it never escapes intrusive action.

IV   REALITY

The tail, the waist, the nose turret or the ball gunner,
Using the sight with floating reticle
Has only, if his work is properly done,
Has only to press the trigger. The enemy explodes in the air.
It is all so fast sometimes
Neither pilot nor gunner can see the result,
Until, far up and away
Banking over, high above the blue ocean
They glimpse far below pieces of plane
Drift idly, suspended in the air.
But reality is there.
Death is the reality in this case,
Love is the reality of St. Theresa,
Identification is the reality of Boehme,
For Blake innocence and experience
Were indistinguishable in mystical affinity,
Our enemy pilot was dead by a death-dealing pounce
Of superior machinery and superior manoeuvre and aim—
But what Chance was there!—
For in battle, as if man were made of adrenalin
There is no time for fear or fault, for faith or fame
But pilots say it is all like a football game.
Back on the carrier their hearts may pound,
After the event, when significance comes,
But up in the air intense and free
Controlled and able,
Perfectly secure,

What is the end of a man
You never saw before,
You never see?

It is the end of this man whose life yours never touched,
Of whose existence you never knew,
Young man, young man,
Whose floating corpse you will never view,
Whose friends you also slew,
It is the end of this man,
Or let us say it is the end of Man
Christ shed his blood for,
He shed His blood for you.

He knew you, savage trickster,
Your accomplished guile,
The total ignorance of your intelligent blasphemy,
The evil that is ineradicable
He died to show.

He would redeem the enemy airman's blood-muffled scream,
He would redeem the pride of your indifferent victory.

Is there any doubt that Christ was the most aesthetic man?
As aestheticism is a part of philosophy,
Philosophy a part of life,
Life action, for even the Nirvana-seeker still breathes,
And Stylites pulls up food in a basket,
So Christ contemplated the ultimate origin,
But originated the ultimate rules of action.
All things are interlocked, interlaced,
Interinvolved, interdenominated.
The pilot who pinched himself in his bomber,
Because only a year ago he was a boy in school,
Hardly realizing the magnitude of his change,

Was only one of a squadron,
A flying integer in a welter of heterogeneity.
Christ belonged to the Jewish race
But Chinese and Japanese speak to Him now.

The poet is a man of sense
Who handles the brightness of the air,
The viewless tittles he dandles,
Timelessness is his everywhere.

His blood is in the rose he contemplates
The blood of the rose reddens in his mind,
The poet is master of presences,
He is the insight of the blind.

Poetry is so mad and so kind
It is so majestic an inventive surprise,
Is it any wonder that in it
The spirit of man arise?

ON SHOOTING PARTICLES BEYOND
THE WORLD

*"White Sands, N.M. Dec. 18 (UP).   'We first throw a little
something into the skies,' Zwicky said.   'Then a little more,
then a shipload of instruments—then ourselves'."*

On this day man's disgust is known
Incipient before but now full blown
With minor wars of major consequence,
Duly building empirical delusions.

Now this little creature in a rage
Like new-born infant screaming compleat angler
Objects to the whole globe itself
And with a vicious lunge he throws

Metal particles beyond the orbit of mankind.
Beethoven shaking his fist at death,
A giant dignity in human terms,
Is nothing to this imbecile metal fury.

The world is too much for him.   The green
Of earth is not enough, love's deities,
Peaceful intercourse, happiness of nations,
The wild animal dazzled on the desert.

If the maniac would only realize
The comforts of his padded cell
He would have penetrated the
Impenetrability of the spiritual.

It is not intelligent to go too far.
How he frets that he can't go too!
But his particles would maim a star,
His free-floating bombards rock the moon.

Good Boy! We pat the baby to eructate,
We pat him then for eructation.
Good Boy Man! Your innards are put out,
From now all space will be your vomitorium.

The atom bomb accepted this world,
Its hatred of man blew death in his face.
But not content, he'll send slugs beyond,
His particles of intellect will spit on the sun.

Not God he'll catch, in the mystery of space.
He flaunts his own out-cast state
As he throws his imperfections outward bound,
And his shout that gives a hissing sound.

WAR AND POETRY

To make a poem cased as honey in a comb,
For it seems pure to be so held.
And of our vocal thrusts, our dispersed days
How to draw all together to a purity,
A rarity? The war was rot of imagery
And bought us off with mammoth extravagance,
That big bad dream of bad small boys.

The poem should be the things we lost, the heart
Of heavenly integers, shells on the sea shore,
Red leaf of Autumn, red bud of Spring,
Soft touch of flesh, nude touch of dream,
Imprisonment of the escaped personages
Valued as historic messengers, elected
Testaments: the poem should atone.

No eclectic dialect, no feverish impishness
Should wrest from flesh nor take from us
The powerful bent; no histrionic extravagance
Conceal the central impetus.
All should be calm, massive, and perpend
The welfare of the inner ecstasy,
Inviolable voice of universal form.

CHOOSING A MONUMENT

Two Brothers and a Sister

MAY

The time is ripe. The land will never go higher.
I have studied all the angles of South Western Law
And believe we should sell our ancestral land.
It is an island of flat land, a desolate waste,
With no grass, no water, only a guess of oil.

ROGER

We should sell it now while the price is high.
We are the third generation of inheritance.
Our grandmother, in a mood of the last century,
Bought sight unseen this domain in the South West
Against the better judgment of our grandfather.
It is a grassless, or almost grassless parcel
Surrounded by thousands of acres of wasteland,
Owned by one man; he alone wants the central part.
We have covered the taxes with the grazing rights
Many years now, having never seen the land itself.

PHILIP

Is it not strange the breakless passage of time
And that we have grown into the world's estate
With this odd inheritance in the desert? This captious
Acquisition? This improbable Eden of belief?
By what whim did our Mid Western grandparents
Think to build a chance Eden in those far reaches?
And gave their hard dollars as light-hearted spendthrifts
To the first fellow who told them a fabulous tale?
Time is a passage over the bones. Time is inheritance.
The land of distant vision went to their children,
Our parents. Time passed. Time is the arch devil.
Time is the passage over the bones. Time is inheritance.

We are full of blood now; all that is left in a sense
Of the last century is the legal fact of ownership.
We did not ask for this, as we did not ask for our lives.
We did not ask for the responsibility
Of paying taxes on grandmother's dream.
We are the inheritors of the earth, of this earth,
This unlikely dry vastness, unproductive, recondite,
An idea only.

MAY

           I have driven by this remote country
Where only sheep graze. In the surrounding territory
To be true prospectors have posited oil,
Oil men have with their wands waved in air,
Which has raised McDermott's price to five dollars an acre.
For decades the sun has hapless heretofore burned.
McDermott wants to buy the mineral rights. If we strike
Oil, we would get without raising a finger
A small percentage of the fabulous gross proceeds.
We received this for nothing. Times change. It is time to sell.

PHILIP

It costs us nothing to keep what our grandparents left us.
Sheep graze idly, nibbling small tufts, decades pass,
We do not suffer from our ownership.
We have in our minds an unseen rendezvous
Of vast flatlands in the coruscated South West,
A somewhere against industrial mechanization,
All improbabilities of our lives; we have this estate,
A dry land to be sure, a waste land eventless
Of which we dream as of a purity,
Handed down from our mysterious ancestors,
A gift as if life were made of liberty.
Keep the dream. Keep the seeming. Keep the land.
I do not vote for dispossession. I rebel
At the faulty gust of overt opportunism
And I do not believe that we should sell.

ROGER

In the middle course of life, as worldly creatures,
We know that all our works will fail. We pass,
We know that. Our parents lie in Northern graves,
Who bequeathed to us this unseen South Western acreage.

PHILIP

What if the oil oozes up from under the earth
And with an irresistible force enriches us?
Where there is any chance of oil, as a spiritual man
I now speak as the most practical, do not sell.

MAY

It is true they have struck oil in the lot next,
But that is due to a fault not lying in our direction.

PHILIP

God may move the fault. Or if we do not live long enough,
Our descendants generations hence may thank us if astutely
We keep our bond with the past. Invisible tradition
Is a sanction invaluable, a precious hoard. To sell
Is earthy, fleshly, gross; to keep the land of our fathers
Is the least we can do, memorially speaking;
And is an idea spiritually incontrovertible.
As we do not know even the outermost secrets
Of our grandparents (a short time back in history)
Our grandchildren will in turn secrete not ours.
But let the land pass down to them in a chain unbroken,
The land as idea. Unused. Let the sun keep it
In the hot bake and the visionary dryness.

MAY

I can arrange for the transfer. Who cares for a joke?
Grandmother bought it from a slick man in an off moment.
It should have been sold long ago by our father,
It is an absurdity to keep it, the price will go down,

Let McDermott who owns the surrounding territory
Swallow it whole; we maintain the mineral rights,
So what can we lose?

ROGER

                                    I have a proposition.
Our parents lie in the North Country. We feel
In every way we are less able than they were.
They lived in a world not knocked apart as ours is,
Or if knocked apart, not so quashed as ours is.
Let us sell our ancestral inheritance
And build over their graves a monument of marble.
Let us erect in the North Country a sign
That we as loyal, dutiful children admit
In the harshness of these times their magnificence.

PHILIP

I object! I object! Glorification of death!
Is this all we can do with the times we live in?
Death and marble are the symbols of our weakness,
Why do we have to serve and erect them? Better act
In favour of the living. This is the death-wish
Of our civilization right in our family. Vanity
Dandles us. What is so vain as a huge monument?
It is an irreverence to the good gross earth,
The round earth, the whole earth, the sweet, the cold earth
To which our bones are not alien and will return.
Cremation is a better idea, at least fiery and airy,
So that we breathe daily our ancestors, the ancestors
Of all the world: air and the earth have kinship.
But you want a name to undergo a slower change,
The weather to meet rebuke of stone for two centuries
Perhaps. You would sell our true bond with the past,
The dream which, quaint and human, is not penetrable,
The inheritance of a fidelity to an unknown quality,
To serve the earth and a few eyes to a monster.

ROGER

> You are theorizing. All it amounts to actually
> Is practical: money from one pocket put into another.
> The Bible says to honour thy father and mother.
> By selling the land we can praise our parents substantially.
> We will not miss the South West land, and besides
> We retain the mineral rights.

MAY

>   We couldn't afford to drill;
> If others do, we receive an eighth without effort.

PHILIP

> This is all the most shocking materialism!
> True love of parents and ancestors lies in the heart,
> Needs no visible sign. Better keep an irrational heap
> Of sun-stricken earth in a far part of the country
> As a curious, captivating bond of vague memory.
> When we die let it continue to new generations.
> Let them guess at the oddness of continuance—
> A lyrical tradition of ponderable insight.

ROGER

> I want a more tangible sort of monument.

MAY

> I think it would be the nicest thing we could do.

PHILIP

> I realize I am at odds with the majority.
> My wish is for a spiritual monument, useless, sensitive,
> That we die and hand the land down again
> As was done to us. A bond of generations, held
> Together strangely by a timeless waste in the desert.
> But since you are against me, I capitulate
> And follow herewith the will of the majority.

70

ROGER

Then let it be done and let it be done well.

MAY

I shall feel that we have accomplished a sacred duty.

PHILIP

To me the evanescent is more valuable
Than obvious marble. But I will go along with you,
And we shall raise a monument to our ancestors.
Thus, in this small, I see a mirror of great
Occasions. It matters little what is suffered in life,
Whether riches or power prevail, or whether worlds fall.
Whether there is one type of civilization, or another.
The forms of love do not matter, but love matters,
And we three who do not agree, by agreeing
Forge in our fashion an invisible bond—

And the blazing air of the South West surely
Will not deny the impact of the Northern climate
Upon the fleshly vanity of ancestor worship,
And the worms surely shall not care what they eat,
And the stone shall not care what it stands over,
And the seed of man surely shall prevail.

The staple of the mind is curiosity,
The staple of the body sperm; if sperm desists
The laughter of the gods is evident;
It is evident in any case.
Innately cruel, life flings us on the scrap heap.
But common man, like common grain
Is spread by lust about the handful earth
And after twenty-four hundred years of history
We are not advanced beyond the Oresteian trilogy.
Yet man is sustained by curiosity
Which, accounting for his mental precocity,
Saves him from sloth by thinking
Up new ways to keep himself from sinking.
This animal is badgered by his brains
Which ge not better for his pains
In architecture, sculpture, painting or poetry,
Although by the arts he seeks that clarity
Through imagination which would order experience,
But the orderly is an offered truce
Until the warfare of chaos begins again
And another poet takes up hurricane pen
To justify the impossible
Subliming scholar, mystic, or arcane apostle
As evidence of man's mastery over nature,
Or by flaunting the great dramatists
He will hold that the freedom of the will persists,
Or by turning his gaze upon God Almighty
He pulls man up by bootstraps in his sight.
Against the background of eternal void
As against the certainty of our destruction,
Man is a rabid creature for belief
And the artist actually sets himself up as thief
Of God's prerogative to be the maker.
The artist is his own butcher or baker.
Actually, he is a kept lighthouse keeper

Who will offer his light to the tall voyeur.
Native to him is the itch of curiosity;
Everything beyond heaven and earth he will see.
He will even see an angel in a tree.
He will embody his visions with authority
And chide us into delectable mazes
That must surely amaze and daze us.
Man is best when he is full of spleen.
Then he can tell the truth of what he has seen.
Artist likewise when they strike at the radex
Are better than when bending on willows
Or when giving the head to airy pillows.
Even if they cut, or watered the root reality
They would kill or nourish an ambiguous tree.
The vision of the artist when it is violent
Is with bitter intention upon mankind spent,
As it was in the case of El Greco
When he had the vision of Toledo
Or if you can't see in the religiosity
Read Swift on his own funeral.
Michelangelo had a fierce vision of man,
Or you may prefer Baudelaire or Rimbaud.
Hopkins was his own caged skylark
Whose best bars were the ruinous dark.
His own spindrft gaze toward Paradise,
Crane tossed the jug of drunkness into the ocean.

Philosophers are at a grave disadvantage
Loping along on the prose of a Kantian age;
It is still prose in Aristotle and Plato.
And prose is prose and prose is slow.
Nietzsche lastly danced like a Superman
In orgiastic revels or revenant poetry.
After the philosophers have parched the verbs
Until their feet are slow and halting
And after they have trounced the nouns and noumena
They are still the poor forked creatures

Whether they were existentializing,
Whether Groddecking, or gestalting,
They are still on the road to dark doom death
With no ultimate truth in their philosophy.
Hear, hear, all you who read philosophy
And you who are wisdom-loving compositors,
The ultimate secrets of language are inexplicable
As is the ultimate secret of thinking.
It may be that the leech gatherer by the lonely moor
Which is to say the mechanic in the aircraft factory,
Turning his bolts in the desuetude of hours, and of years,
Ununderstanding of the gigantic implication
Of which his wrenching is the implementation,
May be nearer to the truth than you will ever be,
May by his innocence outdistance knowledge,
His ignorance the badge of his humility
More valuable than the arrogance of aerial theorists.
The intellectual man may be an offense to heaven,
A vile excresence and sport which nature permits
In her own wisdom, approached by the meek and simple,
Approached only by the broken, the lonely, the sufferers,
It is to these we must go to learn wisdom.
The babe in the manger put to shame the king in the
    temple.
In the lonely manger an ancient story is told
Which baffles the intellect, exposes the haughty brains
And levels the arrogance of fritillary man.

The musician is endeared to mankind because
By the ironic nature of his medium
He has bottled up words with all their fuzz
And given us a madman's immediacy,
We do not have to think, all we have to be
Is to be: music is like an air drink.
Music is thought in its percipiency,
Heaven is somewhere near to harmony,
Which is a long way off from mortality.

Now we come to the type called scientist,
A race of measurers with no further wish,
Who are so far from the truth of nature confounded
That they know what the inside of an atom is
And will not rest content until they pound us
All into the earth with bombs and there impound us
Awaiting the biggest bomb of all, man's final hiss;
Their brains can hardly wait to arrive at this.
Instead of going to the root of man
They choose to go to the root of matter,
Thus love and hate they have lost wholly
And would not care or dare to ingest a soul;
They have no spleen, and they have no pity
But bomb the people and radiate away a city.
The delicacy of their intellectual perceptions
Is only exceeded by the depth of their deceptions.
By brain power alone they can operate,
Too cold for love, too cold for hate,
Not comprehending the best interest of the state
And of the deep needs of man insensate.
These men have exalted the brain too much,
Have measured the world, only the world as such.
They are the positive evidencers of evil,
The sin of acedia is really what they deal in.
They will have to learn to measure less
And that the heart of man is the measureless,
Not space, time, energy, continua, quanta,
Else in sloth they must surely wander
To falsehood's ungainly stance the panders.
I recognize my bias in this letter
And take with one hand what I give with the other.
Who will say what's false, what is true?
The scientists are responsible in what they do,
It only seems more monstrous that they do it
When death usurps what fuller life was intended.
And so to make distinction of the rubbing trees.
Often in the night when the wind will wake

I will wake, and in near distance an unnatural sound
Will come of two huge branches rubbing together.
It is a strange sound of constriction, and necessity,
A kind of forced rhythm, an urgency of fault.
Left alone in their uninterrupted growths
The huge branches do not quarrel, but the wind
Exacerbates their potential incompatibility,
And then all night they sing their raucous song.
Both are from the same trunk and the same tree,
As it is with science and with poetry.
Both are part of man's estate and effort,
Both come from the trunk, the root, the seed of man.

I do not set myself up to be a nihilist
Which is to be a negative moralist.
Frankly, I prefer a philosophical anarchist,
Stressing equally philosophy and anarchy.
An anarchist is a supreme individualist,
A man who has not lost his humanity.
A plague on both your houses, says he,
Or nowadays it is on all three.
His very helplessness is his lack of defeat.
He can see that Christ was the deepest of the deep.
He can philosophize to a considerable distance
Without philosophizing himself out of existence.
He does not have to belong to any established party
Nor flex the shibboleths of popular art, either.
The anarchist is bound to live in poverty
In a society arranged as is our society,
But he can live in human dignity,
He can love man, he can be free,
A passionate man to a passionate degree.

I am not such a philosophical anarchist
But as a symbol him I see
As the radical preserver of what in mankind is free;
As lover, though the outlaw, of the best,

The incurable minority representative
By example teaching the mass how to live,
Who resides in a deep authority,
A residence that is tax- and psyche-free.

If it seems that I minimize the brain
It is in deference to mind, most to spirit.
It is that everywhere there is paradox.
The mind is known as a wiry, wary fox
Can escape all impositions of the absolute,
So he thinks, slink through the last gate,
And I honour him the keenness of his eyes
But I have seen him in his last surprise,
Cornered in a field, his leg in a trap
A big farmer with a club and a gun
Either which way he jumps to smash him,
Even as he tries to gnaw through his leg.
The last gesture of his futility
Argues a similarity in mentality.
Fly the mind to the heights of the air
It must inter-imagine its own despair,
The hunter will crush its ultimate distinction
In the gross inhumanity of extinction.
The business, makeshifts, purposes and powers
Of the mind are stays for some hours;
The irony is that we think they are ours.
The mind is crafty, but it eludes us,
Plato does, Buddha does, Angelus Silesius.
The term that is sager, is safer, is nature,
The voyage, the temple, the rage and the lure.

There is one subject that I do not tire of,
It is the subject man should not write on,
That is, if life were a dream of euphoria
We would not have schizophrenia or paranoia,
Properly not, not have rigorous breath,
We would not be smashed in the face by death.

77

We would not have death as a heavy pall
And conscience of the race upon us all.
But we do have it, we none of us escape it,
Eye susceptive to it on every page.
Dry, inescapable, absolute and specific
This dull word has the charm of the mephitic
And by a twist in our times rife, life
Becomes death because death has become life.
You cannot see a young woman fair and walking
Without feeling the bones beneath her breast,
Nor hear a statesman or a poet talking
Without thinking of Lear haranguing the heath.

The mystery of poetic creation, or
Creeping up on a dark cave at night,
Or being within, but not knowing, a hive of light—
The approach is significant, the stance pure
While the reality is all midnight, or all azure.
To describe and place a poetic state of mind
Would be an elegant statement in its kind:
Mysterious seizure is what it is, it is
Adjunct to no finality, finality itself,
The withholding of trance within the trance,
The deep-sunk life and liveliest dance.
Poetic creation is therefore ultimately mysterious
And the girded mind, with all its moods fused
Extrudes a gift in the free air of chance
Making with lunges and curvets, evasions and frolics
Words to imagine the unimaginable, a holy
Fire: it is the protean heart yet unfixed.

There exists the idea that originality is
Prettification, fancification of the new;
Repetition is represented to be
Myopia of an estuary,
But, look beyond at Drake's Bay,
Beyond, beyond, see the blue Pacific sea

Overwhelming itself with its sole self,
The repetition of a motile continuity;
A few hundred years that Drake came in there
Are as a few days in the windy air:
Even the strangeness is an eternity,
Of high winds without clouds, high sea
Knocking about high cliffs, but eye
Perceives the vast imperturbability.
One of the grandest of nature's evocations
Is the male bull Sea Lion of enormous size
Honking the air as he climbs on the flat rock
To sun himself majestically there;
While under gigantic cliffs in
Shallow water, over the sandy places
Small seals loll on their backs in play
Or poise upright, their heads out of water
Rather like men treading water.
Cormorants only in their hunting flights
See them in the close bight of Reyes Point.
Powerful is the continuity of the seal
Who suffers no problem of the real
But for endurance through the centuries and waters
Is evidence outwitting slaughters.
Patience and grace joined with ungainliness
Instruct in the functions of like manliness
Which, amphibious to spiritual potentiality,
Must lead us to grace on the rocks of its sea.
The ruthless laws of nature they obey
Which are to get fish, to beget, and to slay.

The mind can run as it will over time
Bearing the dimmest memory of pre-human time,
Or if not memory, imagination can feel
The ancient geologic Triassic landscape
In the Petrified Forest of northern Arizona,
Forming in the vast primeval washes
Fossil ferns in shale in the mineral underground.

Here colour and music are equable,
Jasper, chalcedony, carnelian, and agate
Or onyx, apple-green chrysophrase
Speak to the late, the dry and the high air
Just as music speaks; deep underground
The silica into the wood tissues seeped,
One hundred and fifty million years ago,
Silica from volcanic ash releasing to the eye
The startling panorama of the Painted Desert,
While slowly impregnating each cell of the wood
The trees became then colourful logs of stone,
As force uplifted the Colorado River plateau,
From sea level to a mile above the sea.
In remote and ancient times the rhythms
Of the earth in its convulsive mountain births
Shook the petrified logs deep underground.
These seismographic and ordered impulses
In the strange regularity of their natures
Broke the logs in their deep burial vaults
In exact lengths, like measure in music.
While forests now above ground, horizontal,
Show the precise lengths of an orchestrated,
Vast musical utterance of the creative earth.
Veritably to the eye shows a master music
Resolute, fixed, incomparably final
(Yet only final-seeming to our finite eye)
In the live, delirious air of the Arizona earth.
The stones when crushed and examined
Are void of colour; the light and wave length
Of mineral content amaze the eye with colours,
Brittle, subtle life fixed in the dead centuries,
The sun and the eye brilliantly conspiring.

What is art? There is a line fluid and fine
Between will and destiny. Even this line
It is unlikely to determine with accuracy
Whether you follow, or whether it follows you.

Will is a demon, the driving ego;
Destiny, the fate of the times surrounding you.
Between these two there is high drama yearly,
Art a momentary resolution in growth.
Will is eyelight of old ancestors' faces,
Their silence in past centuries made manifest,
Their separateness become a new unity,
Their essence born in a fresh conception.
Secret in your strange, potential recesses
They speak, back to uncontrollable Adam.
Will is inseparable from individuality,
The vocal individuation, uniqueness of the flesh.
The artist escapes neither his times nor his art;
The result is a relative capability.
It has been averred that had Dante appeared in Italy
Fifty years later, or earlier such a like time,
We would not be availed of the Divine Comedy,
Or open it in an unimaginable form:
That wreath is laid upon the brow of destiny
While universal acclaim goes to the great maker.
Likewise it would seem impossible for Shakespeare
To perform in our own times; superior to his,
So that his mastery took two centuries of proof,
He yet in his raucous day drew all together
In secular breadth different from Dante's depth
And mirrored for us the world of man and nature.
The peculiar and secret nature of his will
Is yet an enticing mystery to contemplation,
While the mere execution of his perfections
Startles us in the odds of our foreign lassitude,
Yet in this case the potentiality of chance,
The growing, wide, lusty life of the Elizabethans,
Lends to the argument of fateful circumstance.

Each age deserves the art it gets, no doubt,
Each civilization puts on its own peculiarity,
Each artist, a spectacle to timely beholders,

Is himself caught in their various pageantry,
He becomes himself but by their grace,
He reflects in his own art his own state of grace.

Descending from these grand exemplars of art
And defenders of the commonalty of mankind,
Suppose any young poet in England or America
In the mid decades of the twentieth century.
What frightful chances hit about his head:
As if he had no will at all, fate it seems
Plays with him as a toy in the winds of years,
Deals him blows, hopes, reverses, possibilities—
His very life will hang on a thread in a war—
Family vicissitude is first then dominant,
Then friends, then enemies, then chancy circumstances,
The comic leer and aspect of a wry economy,
Tragedy in its austere and its lofty essences,
Whirl him on along the course he has to go.
The nihilist professor, the philosophical anarchist,
The spokesman for a communist entity,
The withdrawn poet of a philosophical serenity,
Experimenters of the ever receding advance guard,
Or those who fly into the arms of Mother Church
Are caught by the times they cannot change
And are in their deeds the darlings of the age.
They are no worse off than in other times.
Yet, where greatness strikes into the bone of life,
The artist is the only and true changer of life,
For yet, while he is forged, as has been aforesaid,
The powerful intellect and the shaping imagination
Are man's best leadership and principle of guidance.
The great poet dominates the age, as ever,
Creating its very nature in its retrospect,
Its flavour, its temper, its oddity, its peculiarity.

A LEGEND OF VIABLE WOMEN

I

Maia was one, all gold, fire, and sapphire,
Bedazzling of intelligence that rinsed the senses,
She was of Roman vocables the disburser,
Six couturiers in Paris sat to her hats.

There was Anna, the cool Western evidencer
Who far afield sought surrender in Sicily,
Wept under the rose window of Palma de Mallorca,
For she thought fate had played a child in her hand.

There was Betty the vigorous; her Packard of Philadelphia
Spurred she; she was at home in Tanganyika,
Who delighted to kill the wild elephant,
Went Eastward on, to the black tigers of Indochine.

There was Margaret of Germany in America, and Jerusalem,
Of mild big eyes, who loved the blood of Englishmen,
Safely to voyage the Eros battlements of Europe,
Protectress to be of young and home, massive the mother.

There was Helen the blond Iowan, actress raddled,
Who dared learning a little, of coyness the teacher,
Laughing subtleties, manipulator of men, a Waldorf
Of elegant fluff, endangering to the serious.

There was Jeannette the cool and long, bright of tooth,
Lady of gay friendship, and of authentic song,
Beyond and indifferent to the male seduction
Who to art pledged all her nature's want and call.

There was the sultry Emma of West Virginia,
Calf-eyed, velvet of flesh, mature in youngness,
Gentle the eager learner of nature's dimensions,
Always to her controlling womanhood in thrall.

There was Sue, the quick, the artful, the dashing,
Who broke all the laws; a Villager in her own apartment,
She was baffled by the brains of Plato and Aristotle,
Whose mind contained most modern conceptions.

There was Maxine, a woman of fire and malice
Who knew of revenge and subterfuge the skills,
A dominator, a thin beauty, a woman of arts and letters;
She of many psychological infidelities.

There was savage Catherine, who leaped into the underground,
Her female anger thrown at abstract injustice.
And she could match her wits with international man,
A glory, a wreaker, alas, who now posthumous is.

There was Madge the sinister, who raged through husbands
　　　three.
She was somdel Groddeckian, a spendthrift of morality;
Existentialist that with men was dexterous
And would be in ten years after thirty, thirty-three.

There was a nun of modesty, who with service was heavy
And big with sweet acts all her sweet life long;
Enough wisdom she had for twenty ordinary women
Who percepted love as a breath, and as a song.

II

Where is Kimiko, the alabaster girl of Tokyo,
Living in bamboo among rustling scents and innuendoes,
To whom from Hatteras, the Horn, or Terra del Fuego
Returned as to a starry placement the sea voyager?

Where has time cyclic eventuated Vera
The proud noblewoman of Vienna? Among opera lights
She lived in a gaiety of possessive disasters,
Abandoned to the retaliatory shores of music.

Where is the naked brown girl of the nipa hut,
Under fronds, to Mount Mayon's perfect symmetry,
From the wash of the sea, looking from Legaspi?
Where in nature is this form, so brown, so fair, so free?

Where, who, sold into slavery in white Shanghai,
Walked and breathed in grace on Bubbling Well Road,
Subject to ancient sinuosities and patience,
Whose power was to represent unquestioning obedience?

Where is Hortense, the hermetically sealed?
Where is Hermione, haunted by heavens, who hesitated?
Where is Lucy, of bees and liberty the lover?
Where is Eustacia, of marionettes and Austrian dolls?

III

There were prideful women; women of blood and lust;
Patient women who rouged with scholarship's dust;
There were women who touched the soul of the piano;
Women as cat to mouse with their psychoanalyst.

There were women who did not understand themselves
Locking and unlocking misery's largess yearly;
Fabulous women who could not manumit the world
And babbled in syllables of the past and of money.

There were women committed to sins of treachery
The aborters of privilege and of nature's necessity;
There were the sinners in acedia of frigidity
Who negated even the grossness and grandeur of fear.

There were women without tenderness or pity
There were those more male than feminine men
Who rode the horses of their strident fury,
To whom subtle time made a passing bow.

There were independent women of society
Whose proud wisdom was their father's will.
There were mysterious women, Egyptian as a scarab
To whom scent and sound were a mysterious recall.

IV

Women are like the sea, and wash upon the world
In unalterable tides under the yellowing moon
Whose essential spirit is like nature's own,
To man the shadowy waters, the great room.

They come and go in tides of passion, and show
The melancholy at the heart of fullness,
Time crumples them, these vessels of the generations
Are crushed on the rocks as the green sea urchins.

They are the flesh in its rich, watery symbol,
A summer in July under the tenderest moon,
An island in the sea invincible to touch,
A refuge in man against refulgent ideation.

Women have gone where roll the sea bells
In the long, slow, the wide and the clear waters;
Their flesh which is our love and our loss
Has become the waste waters of the ocean swell.

They are the mothers of man's intelligence
To whom he is held by umbilical time,
And far though he roam, to treat with imagination,
He is brought home to her, as she brings a child.

A MAN OF SENSE

Evil was dangled in front of him like an apple,
A winesap. He saw the apple-crush in the cider mill
Like the mesh of blossom on the trees; draining off
More evil as the amber oozed, he would drink it down,
Becoming a part of the blossom and the fruit;
So surely the wine went back to earth in him.

He became aware of evil in the very air,
In time, and while he breathed the delight of June,
He knew not what to make of the evil of the air.
Things screen us; books do; museums filled with art,
The rich success of shale-stood city towers;
War's bloody hiatus, its true or demented dreams.

To live in luxury, to love the difficult,
And clarify the ways of man to men in thought,
Perturbed by God and evil, but letting them be,
Was what the world allowed him, a special plane,
Genius for friendship with the deft and debonair,
But not to go mad over inscrutability.

Imagination was that formative intelligence
That shaped him less to action than to contemplation;
Imagination it was, the inexhaustible source,
That blessed him in luminous, suspended swirls.
He was the recipient of the ages' thought.
He knew the pleasure of an antique loss.

To a man of meditation the memorable
Makes the marmoreal; skunk cabbages can too.
He is the defender of the library cults;
Cut off from agriculture, and from locomotion
In a sense, his ego distills the fluctuant scene,
And he can be the farmer of Horace undebited.

He is for pure merriment and for pure fun.
A cynical joke with a lavender tinge, or an
Irish bull a yard long, or minuscule bombast in
Disruption of the over or the under dog
Infect the air with his suitable laughter.
Laughter is innocence where before there was none.

Precisely he is mysterious, but offends no man;
Talents he has, that is to have no talent unduly.
He averts from his gaze the awkward, the ugly,
A triumph of sheer character; if he is favoured
It is because the times allowed an elegant fate.
Somebody else made the money, he made the manners.

To be fervent, he thought, is not to be true.
To be detached, the observer, is to be true.
The spectator of life is superior to the actor;
The actor, embroiled, does not control the action.
An impersonal eye controls its speculation,
Losing, apparently, the illusion it is in.

He triumphed, delicately, and walked along the Charles.
The old airs of Paris hung about his head.
There was no use doing anything about man.
In China the rice was coming up again.
The boats turned and curved upon the water
Not knowing the mathematical lines they were making

He thought of poetry, and of St. John the Divine;
He thought he had known, one time, as index,
The voluminous interstices of the Inferno,
The Purgatorio, and lessly the Paradiso.
It was not this that was to be his guide.
It was a dream, a secret, a pure idea in time.

He was not a clear soul;
Clarity, perforce, was juvenile.

Often he had thrown himself away
To be sure he was not there to stay.

Espousing the inextricable
Made his temerity with it immiscible.

He sought in everything quality,
Which deviates into policy.

Every action involves criticism
For not being another action.

And every criticism is an instinct
For being in the inner self.

And every effort is a struggle
To evaluate and predict.

And every man loves and loses
In the guilt of experience.

He would not accept any definition of taste
Knowing that change was certain to violate it.
To live in a fluid ambience of the possible
Brought him joy; he gave it back the tentative.

To evade the substratum of one's life,
Those fixed and barnacle-encrusted pylons,
Was not a linguistic feat, but a conceptual.
Water can look like air; disturbed, it becomes flighty.

He had rejected the romantic, as was expected.
Time was when he gorged on gorgeous effect
And never understood, so stuffed, the spectacle.

What then one could not command or do
One said time's perspective would surely show.
That devil of lovers would ruin and debase

An ancient menace which exalted to confound.
At least time would make plain the issue,
Time tragedian become time comedian.

But see his corpse in the ground,
Be sure some massive stain will adhere to it.

But see his soul ascend,
Be sure in the air he will not quite see it.

The very present world was pat.
A classicist. He would get along with that.

If this was to be classical,
To accept a golden evenness
And ease the tension off the eyelids,
Order the blood, be well balanced,

He approved a modern classical stance
And thought, by St. George, that he had it.
Certain dragons of recalcitrant years
He had conquered, and was glad of it.

It was his doughtiness to imagine pure harmony,
Holding the past in fee, the future not fearing,
Walking by water of suicides, swimmers, and sailors,
Dealing out his rich increase on the air
In private meditation: a whole man,
Wholeness describing imaginary society.

If it was Athens he thought he was in,
It was cool and clean, knowledge after tragedy,
And if the ideal Christian commonwealth
It was a prized and inner unity,
And if it was the actual world he was walking in
He made it in his senses by imagination free.

THE VERBALIST OF SUMMER

I

The verbalist, with colours at his hand,
In the events and size of volant summer,
Thought at the sea's edge
How to wash the sovereign waters;

They were in a grandeur of the actual
And they leaped upon his eyes in tunes
That broke from island hills in blues
And flashed across the waves in mauves.

Is this the sea that balks my verbalism,
The mediator said, by flying hyalines,
Is this sea actual? Is this the real sea?
For he was the register of reality.

Or is it a chasm where old bones are rolled;
Forced peace with roaring rollers made
In the mad tangles of sea bells, fog, fate,
That specific for the forecast of our doom?

Or is it, while his nimble fingers flexed
The dawns, the sunsets of old centuries,
Awaiting the charms of elegance, of synthesis
Which ones to use, which tones to blend,

Is it the subtle messenger of nature
Hidden in the complexity of Psyche
That here appears, and are these bells, these shades
The temper of our mysterious complicity?

Was the water factual? Was it actual?
Did the eyes deceive, and did the senses drown
His too attentive blood in sudden frenzies
That made a music rare and rich in air?

He had the colour harmonies at hand
In the calm vegetation of his eyes;
In the aural cavities of carved sea rock
The rhythmic knowledge of neap certainties.

The verbalist, in all this wealth and scale,
Kept looking at the laughing, dappling water,
Hypnotic to the last, until his vision ceased,
And clearly then he saw that he was natural

To the menacing and the loving sea,
His intellect a super-imposition;
The verbalist sat in dells of verbalism,
As in a flower field, with music in the air,

And he made the sea level with his eyes,
No longer in the power of the imponderables.
All that mystery of the washing waters
Dissolved within his mortal reality.

II

The sea is mine, I am the sea,
For I am human if I am anything,
And I am the master of what I see,
Said to himself the cogent verbalist.

I am what I dream, the waters that I make
Are dreams of summer-scented splendours;
They are the dawns that stir the cormorants
Across the brightening ledges, and the gulls'

Elaborate conclamations. They are the loons'
Curious litanies, and the high osprey's cry.
I dream the waters, and I make the sea
Responsible; for I am what I take and make.

Subjective sea, sea of the deep sea-wish,
Waters of the blood that wash the world,
I claim the element of size and tone
My own, I make the sea, I am the sea;

Stylization of objects, fixation of dreams,
Compendium of imponderables,
Visionary screen on which is played
The magic games of the soul's reality.

So said the viewing verbalist
By the side of the ocean segment,
Mindful and instructed that he
Was, actually, foreign to this element.

And knowing that, where eyes were wide
To so many occult divergencies
His tones and colours were his own
The sundial sea was the plastic timepiece

As it had been when he began his reverie
And would be ten thousand years from now,
A living nature beyond the realm of art,
Try as poetry does to have it poetry.

III

I must begin again, the verbalist said.
The sea is always gettting out of hand;
It is an addict of the summer's chances.
Those air-dances on the water, there, he said.

I must arrange the props, theorize
The distances and densities, defend
The subtlest of shifting elucidations.
The sea is a subject of some malfeasance.

He began to brim with violent intensities.
He saw a savage power, the ships broken up;
He had not thought so changeable a source
Could violate so many presumed images.

Accept the historians too; and of the weather
The weather-makers. And of sea-power
Its expositors and rampant individualists;
And place just so the salmon canneries.

The dullness of the ritual lighthouse keepers;
The thickening of the salt by centuries.
Typhoons, unseen, in the pacific sea;
Scott tying up to the Great Ice Barrier.

He began to think it was too much,
The subject proliferous and cantankerous,
No medicine to the subsuming spirit
Or order, gall to the onlooker, a tempest.

To be didactic about the ocean
Is to be a child, the verbalist said.
What does the child see in the ocean?
He sees the bright pebbles by the shore.

PART III

AN HERB BASKET

We are fighting still to know
What we are doing in writing.
Are we making an engine, making
It go? Are we playing with a balloon?
Are we inviting Heraclitus?
We are fighting: but do we know?

2

Are we questioning the Absolute
With our bones inadequate,
Or, rather, staving in time
With the ancient game of wit;
Or are we, brash expositors,
Mocked by a savage gambit?

3

Are we so devoid of love
As not to see the people on the move?
'What the traffic will bear'
Contains poetic ambiguity.
But what of the gay girl in the grass,
And of that simplicity, Alas!

4

A cereal-fed fat oyster
Kept for a winter dinner
Is an example of sophistication
And a case of debasement.
I would rather have it thinner
With some sea water in my dinner.

5

I praise the wayward mind,
Not the prancing realist.
These glints have got into science:
They thought a new shoot in quanta,
Where it was an old Greek dance,
A Pan-pipe invention of the hills.

How to put it that boys are coming on
Whose mothers soon back were small girls.
A frank perspective of the middle way.
The old see us as hobblers,
Who see the children dabblers,
Soon, soon we will be old men.

How many rages of the sea's
Contagion take lives away;
They mistook a halcyon look,
Had not sea-sense to turn about,
When that ruffian arm came sweeping,
And nine lives in the bin in one hour.

Leisure is what we are after,
To think the blood through the veins.
It takes a revolution to sit still.
Charms are beyond the window
And a yellow bird on the sill;
Sage music gleams, come when it will.

The ash can is a symbol of books
Put out as the years go by.
We live to consume ourselves
While time is mysteriously by.
What, for all the talk and frenzy,
Of thoughts uncome-by, not thrown out?

They shoot each other with old guns
In the new wars, in the old wars.
Twice we have seen it in our time.
Conscience in prison held some;
Chauvin too; and some are gone
Under the hill of Marathon.

11

In an extremity of ecstasy,
Against the world of reality,
Two lovers met on Mt. Etna.
And they swore in their singleness
(It was youth they wore and tore)
It was neither Scylla nor Charybdis.

12

There was a blue reservoir
Fitted with jewelled stones,
And in this reservoir a tincture;
The well gave back a gaze.
Many years he tried to fathom it
With his life's stain from it.

13

It was curious how a hand
Had lain upon an arm,
And an arm upon the sky.
And how the sky in turn was God's
Arm upon a conscious hand,
And made it write in love and purity.

14

We sift the canons; imagination
Is a rich lush mesh.
There are three ways to take a bow.
One is not to have appeared;
One is to pull the *deus ex machina*;
And one is not to leave the stage.

15

He got the whim of the ether.
The noble dream one way,
The other the pixie glance.
Oedipus the fool of his blindness,
Of his vision the fool Falstaff.
He, astride, by both bemused.

It is possible to wipe the slate clean.
The senses require an anarchy.
Knowledge is not something stated,
But a red dream; to ignore
The mean is to defy the norm,
And wash the world to the newly seen.

To get him off the ship
By stealth, in the night's dead watch,
Was practicality and idealism
Combined, a sailor saved
From sailors, off Mindanao,
In a blue, Filipino, outrigger canoe.

We forget gargoyles are rainspouts.
We forget rains are gargoyles
Carved by the artisans of summer;
We behold the cathedral of the heavens
Whose composition threatens iridescence.
We suggest. But we forget too much.

It is said that time destroys grief
And this, to be true, must be admitted.
But when it is destroyed
We wish to have our grief again
For we realized in our pain,
Our loss, the surge of life.

The trees are a mode of appearance
And have in them a gloomy darkness
Where I like to walk in thought
With my dark charges; even as
I lurked in youth in moody woods
With my blooded destinations.

CONCORD CATS

The soft cat and the scratchy cat
Have milk in cold blue plates.
Then, in evenings, star-cool evenings
Equal to their reticence,
Emblems of independence,

These China cats, of black and white,
Will go on planetary pads
Uphill, where crouch
On eighteenth-, seventeenth-century
Houses, the graves of Concord.

By pious inscriptions
That antedate the Revolution
They see, through eyes cold and chaste,
The scratchy cat, the soft cat,
With humour old and Oriental,

That nature is meant for poise.
Battles, bloodshed, death,
Are men mirroring time,—
The stars blue, the night paling—
Are data. Imperviousness. Integrity.

PHOENIXES AGAIN

In a glow of deepest day
In a garden of peonies
Two poets come to pray
Inventoried the meanings.

They sat under a myrtle
In the spring of the year
Reading The Phoenix and the Turtle
In a green amphitheatre.

They were amazed, they were delighted
And held its secrecy up
As wine in the blood lighted,
With time of the world to sup.

One said, I will find the meaning,
I will invent the key
To open the veiled seeming
Of this subtle mystery.

The other, much the same inclined,
Said, a thing so beautiful
Should be ultimately fruitful,
Understandable by the mind.

These two young poets in their grace
Loving the garden syllables
Said in that flowery place
Vows like wilful bells.

There was a god behind them,
A god of cloudy piety
Who could hold a flower by the stem
Without anxiety.

This was the flower of great price,
The flower never broken.
And the god of snow and of ice
Laughed at the vows taken.

He was a god beyond enticement,
A magical ancient, hieratical,
Whose soul was made magical,
And whose secret was musical.

Subtle, and of an airy presence,
He was an enemy of sense,
A master of nuances,
Vanquisher of pretense.

The mind in its logical frames,
The will in its towering forms,
Performed through the years their games
In nature's blood and nature's storms.

Two decades almost have passed and gone
But the meaning is rare and strange
As it was that fluent day
When hopes were first emblazoned.

Still the cold god hovers there
Absolute, strange, and specific,
Though the years have worn bare
The mind, accustomed and honorific.

And two poets twenty years later
Sustained by love, or faith, or lust
Must submit themselves to something endless,
Must bow to spirit, though in mind they trust.

CODA

As a day deploys, so a year recedes.
As a decade changes, so ages change.
As the heart yearns, so the bones disperse,
But the spirit lives in mystery.

I would be her celebrant,
I would in famous gyres
And words of music true and full
Address her in their funeral figures,

And I would strew upon the air
Of this mid-time, while strong in blood,
Mellifluous marks of devotion
On skies of remarkable striation.

And I would with my praise
Subdue the mind to flesh's parity
And as that goes, conclame
Order, calm, and luxury.

LINES TO AN OLD MAN

When you were young and the land was large
The world was all a gay abandon.
Now memory is the only largeness.
In the eye of memory how the world is slight.

Yours was the rush of earth's infinitudes,
You seized your blood on battlements of Asia.
And yours was the hush of silent contemplation,
And yours was the pledge of the mind's naked source.

How many deaths control each circling year
And how many stars are broken in the sky
Now that evil has displaced the goodness,
Now that there is nothing left to do but die.

You who were drenched in love are clenched by death
As old age hastens his comic suspiration,
And you who grasped the actual realities
Have become parcel of an ancient allegory.

Then let us praise you as an example of nature,
And as is man's need, hallow your icy head
With all the faith there is in the living,
And all the folly there is in the dead.

TO MY SON, AGED FOUR

Those eyes that are like mine, that gaze,
The laughing instep, all the learning,
Trouble me with the night's surprise,
For time is turning, turning.

I see in those eyes like gain
I had when mine were brimming.
And what is the whole of life
But a drowning in the act of swimming?

Mind is a most delicate evidence.
Not a soul has seen it yet.
And yet I think it is dense,
Although of great expense.

I suspect it of all trickery,
The master of the greatest paradoxes.
It is the historian of the world,
Crafty and foxy.

Old entablatures in Venice remind me
Of the mind of Tintoretto or Veronese.
These came to a watery nothingness
But for the golden paint I see.

I think there is no mind at all,
Perhaps, but only desires and faiths,
And the great capability of art
Which shows us forms, divine.

ORDER AGAIN

I return to order as one ailing.
I become the thing I long for and desire.
I am a momentary order
Speaking harmony before disaster.

It is something to have forsaken faiths.
It is much to see every eye afresh.
It is a kind of resurrection
To have outlived each prejudice.

Now the sun is a misty master,
And the air is a moist forgiveness.
Now I believe I am free,
Who wished to believe himself free.

To speak for order in a time of chaos
Is the tough, root rights of man,
And rite of undeniable, tensile strength,
To those who have hidden springs.

Let then a symphony begin,
And subtle sweep, and waiting string,
That the fine harmonies in-ring
And the soul dwell in immaterial things.

And let us be as we were once,
Before experience and time compelled us,
Let us revel in the pure delight
Of the first kingdoms of our sight.

I return to order where I was
Before the necessity of the world
And I dream upon that kingdom
As the drowning see the skies above them.

1

A dog, dead forty years ago, unearthed
Under the kitchen by the furnace men,
Mummified like a man, wraith-like as a cat,
Maybe a dog, maybe a cat,
Tells us what we knew a long time ago.

2

Returning to a cabin in the mountains,
On a headland, overlooking a far blue sea,
One looked at the bed where young love
Once endured youth,
As foreign as if it had been imagination.

3

The fine-grained cheek of Aunty Vine,
Who is eighty-four, upon whose
Benign head one looks in a kind of
Bemusement, brings back
The dense, false world when one was secure.

He made furtive marks on paper,
Evasive shoots, each for a thousand loves,
As if to defeat time,
Fullness addressing carelessness.

As if to get himself back!
Yet only caring a little,
To catch a little evanescence;
To hail indifference.

He made them sportive and casual,
Signs of largeness, the least
Gesture to mean a flambeau,
A fig for a seduction.

A pleasure against a threat
Of crystallization! The amorphous
Caged and confined, a shoot of life;
Let Homer lie, let Dante sleep.

Intelligence in minute obliqueness!
His meticulous, sporadic strokes,
A lightning of imagination,
Stood for the century's fevers.

Who can conjure up the sensation
Of unity with the world?
Who can feel the world a harmony
In the eye of the Almighty God?

Then in the buckle of tragedy,
In multifarious instances,
May not a furtive mark on paper
Speak for the dignity of man?

TO ONE, WHO, DEAD, SEES HIS POEMS IN PRINT ONE HUNDRED YEARS LATER

Immortality is colder than I thought,
A partial insight on a page.
The fervour of my bloody thought
And blood, blurred for an age.

I thought my lust was absolute,
I thought my invention elegant.
You do not get my drift,
I take your crooked stance.

I spoke my love out in a rage,
Emptying the purple vessels.
Better to be shifting still
In waters of the unsatisfied.

Who should have wrought sound clear,
Who should have unified the syllables
With the century worsening,
Death astrew on the sea.

MOTION AS GRACE

It was a motion across a new room,
A deviate way, a pause, a turn of the hand,
And turn of the head's patrician elegance,
Indicated a royal afternoon.

To lie stubborn, toes up, renowned
Among the shucks and stones of time,
Eventual, formally breathless,
Makes comic the gentle afternoon.

I saw Ilaria del Caretto
Once, in her marble rightness and primness,
Whose sculptor refreshed my sense
Of a soft Italian afternoon.

No, do not move, for you shall not.
Let the mind with time abide alone.
But turn your delicate head this way,
But move, and gracious is this afternoon.

So shall the ecstasy of sense
Receive a subtle strength; so find
An amiable charm; and so our love
Shall be and take the soul of motion.

PLEASURES OF THE MORNING

O that large dream of masterful events,
The take-off from the daffodil!
Where upon the edges of the air
The blue jay, spike of colour, a clash
Of sense, this heretic, upsweeps
To fasten on the bough his tactic blue.

He brought me back from vagueness to the real.
I had been thinking of the yellow jonquil,
Up-borne from thence to paradoxes of the vast,
Lost, daft, adrift in ethereal endlessness
Where pageants of supremacy, lucky actions
Brazen on the air their militant tattoos.

I lived in the large airs of ancient frenzies,
Perhaps, with time's embattled strategies,
The visitations of the springs of action,
Man in his tempest sacrifice to spirit,
The daemon driving through the springing air,
No surfeit, aspirations, endless treacheries.

In the amazement of abrading, bookless transfer
Knitted in the strictest synthesis
Against the garden sweetness, the enlivening air,
The sent bird defends against the general.
I am biffed upon the eyeballs, I see knowledge,
How neatly tucked in, how tensile, how pure.

I have watched their caution over months,
Extending upward and across the air:
What faith is theirs, what patience!

The green shoots of the new year
From where I trained them to the rusty fence
Believe in the wind, in space itself.

They bend out as if they could not bend so far.
They strain upward with a sturdy delicacy.
It is their quiet assurance that moves me.

How could they lean across the air so far
Or push so almost straight upright
Without a strange and surcharged certainty?

They know the wind will one day on their tendrils
Push a puissant force, fixing their green fingers
Just long enough to close and keep.

They feel that space must give itself away,
Gifted space, presenting some fine object
Keenly, closely, surely to cling to.

Beyond aesthetic blond sight my blood
Abounds in love of your intent
As in the vine I await the grape.

GREAT PRAISES

Great praises of the summer come
With the flushed hot air
Burdening the branches.

Great praises are in the air!
For such a heat as this
We have sweated out our lives toward death.

I used to hate the summer ardour
In all my intellectual pride,
But now I love the very order

That brushed me fast aside,
And rides upon the air of the world
With insolent, supernal splendour.

THE GREAT STONE FACE

No way to outwit the grim-faced mountains,
Except by moving upon the earth.
Witless work! Late I come back
To see them massive in their frames.
Twenty-five years is the time of separation.

Little has changed. I think I even
Have not changed, and am as far from finality
As when, youthful and dour, I trudged
On, told the lonely peaks of doubt.

Agility of mind is its own commitment,
No victory. The stones are committed to silence,
Even as we. The chill, early air of April
Is good as when I first knew it in New Hampshire.

Our times are different. Neither escapes
The grip of nature. I stand here hale
Who stood to these mountains in my twenties.
I see no difference in their attitude.

Poems will invent the new possibilities,
They speak of the passion of man for victory,
For realization, the highest consciousness,
Even Christ's. They are pages strewn on the wind.
They are purities, like this light-stepping, high air.

THE DRY ROT

The fine powder of the dry rot,
A new texture in the heart of the wood,
Crooked my finger as I scooped it out,
The rare old stuff of mankind's dream.

What to do with it? Pure contemplation?
Savage remorse? Illimitible irony?
A cosmetic for the face of Cleopatra?
Time in the blood is this pale substance too.

I mixed it with my sweat, and painted on
My legs and biceps bands of gold.
Sallying forth in the guise of Anthony
I sought the dusky land of sandy Egypt.

With a savage queen I lost remorse;
I threw my manhood down along a gold divan.
With a gesture of defiance and of loss
I met the meaning of the dry rot in that land.

Dig me up, then, in some later century,
Threading the pale sand through your thin fingers.
As you unclothe my bones in scholarship's delight,
Think of dialectic, imagination, the Rose of Venus.

THE SKIER AND THE MOUNTAIN

The gods are too airy: feathery as the snow
When its consistency is just the imagination's,
I recognize, but also in an airy, gauzy way
That it will capture me, I will never capture it.
The imagination is too elusive, too like me.
The gods are the airiness of my spirit.
I have dreamed upon them tiptop dreams,
Yet they elude me, like the next step on the ski.
I pole along, push upward, I see the summit,
Yet the snow on which I glide is treachery.
The gods are too airy. It is their elusive nature
I in my intellectual pride have wished to know.
I have thought I knew what I was doing,
Gliding over the cold, resisting element,
Toward some summit all my strength could take.
The gods are the fascination of the place, they escape
The genius of the place they make. They evade
The blood of our question. Imagination is a soaring,
It never allows the firm, inevitable step.
The gods tantalize me, and the gods' imaginations.
I am thus the captured actor, the taken one,
The used, I am used up by the will of the gods,
I am their imagination, lost to self and to will.
In this impossibility is my humility.

I saw an old country god of the mountain,
Far up, leaning out of the summit mist,
Born beyond time, and wise beyond our wisdom.
He was beside an old, gnarled trunk of a tree
Blasted by the winds. Stones outcropped the snow,
There where the summit was bare, or would be bare.
I thought him a dream-like creature, a god beyond evil,
And thought to speak of the portent of my time,
To broach some ultimate question. No bird
Flew in this flying mist. As I raised my voice

118

35 To shape the matters of the intellect
And integrate the spirit, the old, wise god,
Natural to the place, positive and free,
Vanished as he had been supernatural dream.
I was astonished by his absence, deprived
40 Of the astonishment of his presence, standing
In a reverie of the deepest mist, cloud and snow,
Solitary on the mountain slope: the vision gone,
Even as the vision came. This was then the gods' meaning,
That they leave us in our true humanity,
45 Elusive, shadowy gods of our detachment,
Who lead us to the summits, and keep their secrets.

IMAGINATION

Imagination is a god of fire,
No appeaser or mediator,
Hostile, erradicative.
Come to it, then, nakedly.

You will feel it when your senses fail,
No high thing of the thinking mind.
All's cut down to bone and weeds.
Pride and vanity are fled. Then pure

You are and ready to be ploughed.
You are ready for the fast rebirth.
Imagination is a fire, a plough, or it
Is anything you like to fashion free.

Now wholeness flashes on the vision,
The world is possible again.
You live in passionate happiness,
Not endangered in the inane.

THE DREAM OF TIME

A savage, but a dim milieu.
  Yet imprecision mocks the mind.
  New, powerful wings are over the sea.
  Another year finds nature inexhaustible.

The death-strife, but the living grace.
  I cannot bring it all to mind.
  Just at the height, in the blueberry
  Is the purest paleness ever seen.

A violent grip! A savage mark!
  A rage upon the wind and waters.
  Time shall be put out of mind
  Only when time is inexhaustible dream.

CALLIGRAPHY

The letters themselves wrinkled
Until, with a shock of recognition,
He knew they wanted to be something else.

The crooked 'a's and time-dilapidated 't's,
No longer extruded as things in themselves,
Not round as is the eye of a bird,

Were themselves an expression of nature
Trying to outfly the whole field of writing.
When thought was perfect, would nothing be
        written at all?

Were these scrawls, these so changed syllables,
This script in its puckered individuality
Advancing toward an illegible spirituality?

He felt an analogy with deeper things,
And wondered, as hand trailed off paper,
Can the Soul do without the Body?

Does time struggle to release the being
So that we may never rest in things,
But glimpse ever a higher reality?

The poem then taken off the page,
In some subtle metamorphosis,
Given back, and lived in the hearts of men?

THE LOST POEM

Buried among papers, among savage years,
Irretrievable, the richest poem was lost.
In desperate and frenzied Saturnalias
He sought it even in redemptive hours.
These hieroglyphs, continuous in the mind,
Were dark clouds of knowing and unknowing.
He searched the books again, prodigal time,
For the lost poem of vision and control.

Buried among effects, lost to living language,
The dark secret of its formidable grace
Made anguish frequent for so whole a knowledge,
Forced kinship with disparate phenomena;
As the soul worked in its frenetic passages,
The image of the lost poem, priceless on its paper,
Secreted somewhere in time's croak and chaos,
Bestrode imagination, and made gladness cruel.

It was on that parchment, hieratic, milky,
He wrote the soul's inevitable passion,
And fixed upon the junctures of the spirit
Miraculous juice, else afar, immortal.
It was there the antique harmony prevailed
And there the newest love was real, was true.
And on that imaginary field, the greenest earth,
Evil and good were mated under the sun.

THE HUMAN BEING IS A
LONELY CREATURE

It is borne in upon me that pain
Is essential. The bones refuse to act.
Recalcitrancy is life's fine flower.
The human being is a lonely creature.

Fear is of the essence. You do not fear?
I say you lie. Fear is the truth of time.
If it is not now, it will come hereafter.
Death is waiting for the human creature.

Praise to harmony and love.
They are best, all else is false.
Yet even in love and harmony
The human being is a lonely creature.

The old sloughed off, the new new-born,
What fate and what high hazards join
As life tries out the soul's enterprise.
Time is waiting for the human creature.

Life is daring all our human stature.
personification Death looks, and waits for each bright eye.
Love and harmony are our best nurture.
The human being is a lonely creature.

INTERIOR EVENTS

The best are in the genius nest,
The worst are in the wars,
Universals sit in the flesh,
Particulars burn in the stars.

I will buy you amber wares
And strike the heavens for certainty.
Would you stop time for me
With your gaze moist and early?

And I would abjure philosophy
That's thick and horny,
But you will go your own way
And make me cold and surly.

Let us speak a word so pure,
So featly, and feel so keenly
That the world will be your only praise,
And poetry be your whole meaning.

THE BOOK OF NATURE

[Undercliff, 1952]

As I was reading the book of nature
In the fall of the year
And picking the full blueberries
Each as round as a tear;

As I was being in my boyhood
Scanning the book of the rocks,
Intercepting the wrath to come
Where the hay was in the shocks;

As I was eye-drinking the waters
As they came up Seal Cove
With the eyes of my dazzled daughter,
An absolutist of a sudden grove;

As I was on that sea again
With islands stretching off the sail,
The real sea of mysterious time,
Islands of summer storm and hail;

As I was living with the love of death,
A concentrated wonder of the birches,
Passionate in the shudder of the air
And running on the splendour of the waters;

As I was a person in the sea birds,
And I was a spirit of the ferns,
And I was a dream of the monadnocks,
An intelligence of the flocks and herds;

As I was a memory of memory,
Keeper of the holy seals,
The unified semblance of disparates
And wielder of the real;

As I was happy as the ospreys,
As I was full of broom and bright afflatus,
As I was a vehicle of silence
Being the sound of a sudden hiatus;

As I was the purified exemplar
And sufferer of the whole adventure,
And as I was desire in despair,
A bird's eye in doom's nature;

As I stood in the whole, immaculate air,
Holding all things together,
I was blessed in the knowledge of nature.
God is man's weather.

Then I saw God on my fingertip
And I was glad for all who ever lived,
Serene and exalted in mood,
Whatever the mind contrived.

Then God provided an answer
Out of the overwhelming skies and years
And wrath and judgment then and there
Shook out the human tears.

Printed in Great Britain
at Hopetoun Street, Edinburgh,
by T. and A. CONSTABLE LTD.
Printers to the University of Edinburgh